moja means one

moja means one

SWAHILI COUNTING BOOK

by Muriel Feelings · pictures by Tom Feelings

THE DIAL PRESS · NEW YORK

To all Black children living
in the Western Hemisphere,
hoping you will one day
speak the language—in Africa

the continent of Africa, showing countries where Swahili is spoken

NILE

RIVER

SOMALIA

DEMOCRATIC
REPUBLIC OF
THE CONGO

UGANDA

Kampala ★

KENYA

★ Mogadishu

RWANDA

Kigali ★

★ Nairobi

Bujumbura ★

BURUNDI

+ MT. KILIMANJARO

★ Kinshasa

TANZANIA

★ Dar es Salaam

Z A M B I A

MALAWI

MOZAMBIQUE

Lusaka ★

Zomba ★

MALAGASY REPUBLIC

★ Tananarive

★ Lourenço Marques

introduction

All over the world people speak different languages. Languages differ according to the country or society in which people live. People use numbers for counting, and the words for numbers are from the words of their language. You may know some words from languages other than English, but do you know any words from an African language?

Africa, one of the largest continents in the world, spreads over 11 million square miles. There are about 800 African languages spoken in the many nations of this vast continent. Swahili is spoken across a wider geographical area than any other single language. It is the language of about 45 million people in the eastern part of Africa: in Kenya, Uganda, two-fifths of the Congo, on the coasts of Mozambique and Somalia, in the northern part of Malawi and Zambia, and by the townspeople of Rwanda, Burundi, and in Rhodesia as a language of commerce. It is spoken on the islands off the coast of East Africa such as Seychelles, Kilwa, and the Malagasy Republic. It is the national language of Tanzania. A person from Congo can speak with a person of Kenya, a Tanzanian can talk with a Ugandan or Rwandan. One major importance of learning Swahili is that it serves as a common language and a unifying force among the many varying cultures and countries of Africa.

I lived for two years in Uganda and taught in a high school in Kampala, the capital. I also had the opportunity to travel around Uganda, to parts of Kenya, Tanzania, and Congo, visiting with families in cities and villages throughout the countryside. Though the people in each country were of various ethnic groups and spoke their own language, they also spoke Swahili. Therefore I could communicate with them, though my knowledge of Swahili was limited. I found that in learning this language, I understood more of the culture (the way of life, the customs, values, history) of my people in East Africa.

Africa is the original homeland of about 100 million Black people who live in the United States, Canada, Central and South America, and the Caribbean islands. As our people in the Western Hemisphere learn more and more about our African heritage, we become increasingly proud. Part of our heritage is language. For example, in various Black communities in the United States, many of our people have taken Swahili names, Black students are learning Swahili in schools and colleges, private schools and shops bear Swahili names such as *Uhuru Sasa* (Freedom Now) School and *Uhuru Kitabu* (Freedom Book) Shop.

I have written this book in the hope that young boys and girls of African origin will enjoy learning to count in Swahili, together with gaining more knowledge of their African heritage.

Muriel Feelings

moja means one

1 moja
(mo·jah)

Snowy Kilimanjaro is the highest mountain in Africa.

2 mbili
(m·bee·lee)

Mankala, a counting game, is played by villagers young and old.

3 tatu
(ta·too)

Farmers grow coffee trees in all parts of East Africa.

4 nne
(n·nay)

Mothers usually carry their babies on their backs while walking.

5 tano
(tah·no)

Many kinds of animals roam the grassy savannah lands.

6 sita
(see·tah)

The clothing East Africans wear includes the kanga, busuti, lapa, kanzu, and dashiki.

7 saba
(sah·bah)

The Nile River, which flows between Uganda and Egypt, is filled with fish.

8 nane
(nah·nay)

Busy market stalls are stocked with fruits, vegetables, meats, fish, clothes, jewelry, pottery, and carvings.

9 tisa
(tee·sah)

Men play drums, thumb pianos, bamboo flutes, and other instruments.

10 kumi
(koo·mee)

At night in villages old people tell stories to children around the fireside.

AUTHOR'S NOTE

Kiswahili is the proper name for the language we call Swahili. The prefix *ki* denotes the actual language rather than the people who speak the language. (For example, a person who speaks Swahili would refer to the language spoken by the Ganda people as "kiganda," and to the Luo language as "kiluo.")

Because city life is basically similar around the world, I have not discussed it in this book. My intent rather has been to acquaint readers with what is unique about East African life. It is important, however, that children also learn about African cities, governments, universities, commerce, the arts, and other aspects of African culture.

MURIEL FEELINGS was born in Philadelphia and went to California State College. She has lived in East Africa, where she taught for two years. Upon her return she taught high-school art in Brooklyn. Her first book, *Zamani Goes to Market*, illustrated by her husband Tom Feelings, has received enthusiastic reviews.

Mr. and Mrs. Feelings and their young son Zamani have recently moved to Guyana, where she is working on a new book.

TOM FEELINGS, well-known illustrator and artist, was born in Brooklyn and attended the School of Visual Arts. Mr. Feelings lived in Ghana for two years and has traveled in East Africa. Among the many books he has illustrated is *To Be a Slave* by Julius Lester. Mr. and Mrs. Feelings plan to live in Guyana for the next couple of years and then move permanently to Africa.

H96
FEE

Feelings,
Muriel

72-495

Moja means one

DATE			